Before & After: Poems of Love & Grief
Copyright © 2024 Lisa McAllister

Cover Art from the painting *Mother* by Joaquín Sorolla y Bastida
Cover Layout by Andrew Hilliard
Author Photo by Tim McAllister
Copy Editing by Tiffany Woodley

The interior font used is Garamond
The front cover fonts are Alternate Gothic ATF and Adobe Handwriting
The back cover font is Franklin Gothic ATF

Gnashing Teeth Publishing
242 East Main Street
Norman AR 71960

Printed in the United States of America

ISBN 979-8-9898345-1-8

Non-Fiction: Poetry

Gnashing Teeth Publishing First Edition

Before & After:
Poems of Love & Grief

For Allen

Forward

My 25-year-old son, Allen, said goodbye and walked away for the last time on August 20th, 2019. Later that night, he snorted a lethal combination of heroin and fentanyl off his guitar while sitting in the driveway of his apartment. I woke up to urgent messages and voicemails from the hospital. I rushed there only to be told that my first born was gone.

It took many months to get my words back and I couldn't listen to music for over a year. In the car, I listened to radio plays about hard-boiled detectives written and performed by people long dead. I let the words wash over me while I sat in traffic and sobbed. At home, my husband and I lay in bed and watched B monster movies about killer tomatoes and sexy ladies in space. The scripts were silly; nothing was meant to be serious. Sometimes I would fall against the wall in the hallway on my way to the bathroom because the weight of what I had lost was too much to bear.

Allen was a musician, and I knew I couldn't ignore music forever. As I slowly let it back into my life, he returned to me as my personal DJ, playing me songs on satellite radio he wanted me to hear or, sometimes, the songs I needed to. Through music, little by little, my words returned to me, and I started to write poetry again.

Allen was born of poetry, named after Ginsberg and brought up by two writers in a home of words. Even now, to use words to conjure him seems insufficient, even puerile. Yet, his spirit urges me on. Parents who lose children are everyone's worst nightmare. It can be an isolating and lonely place and I've only gotten through it with love from those who knew my son and the thought that maybe he is somewhere else, watching and playing music and laughing. Maybe he *is* music. Maybe he *is* laughter.

These poems reflect a life lived in hope, in love, and ultimately in grief, a life forever split into before and after. It's how I designate time now. They tumble back and forth through time–from when I was a struggling new mother to staggering through an unimaginable loss–and in doing so, they hopefully give the reader a glimpse of how capricious life really is.

Almost five years into this new reality, I'm still broken (and always will be). Yet, I'm always reminded of the Leonard Cohen quote, "There is crack in everything. It's how the light gets in." Occasionally, there is light for me now and that is enough.

Table of Contents

Genesis

a story that's still being written
preface
a curse we called down on ourselves
        when we sat in blanket fort rubbing hands over
each other's shorn heads
        we talked in baby language
and secret ancient charms swelled in tenement apartment
                --blues lyrics and the sound of a snow plow--
oceanic pull
some genesis
masterful first line of a novel
infant skull squall
slipped as easily as a key into lock of first real house
                found without metal detector
                traced without mystic palm reader
                tattooed on soul without gun or ink
the shape, the contour of face in sleep
the arc of bare foot
some might call it love at first sight
a thing that could happen to anyone
when we know we opened a door
and cosmic light shot out
and enveloped us
and shook us up to space in astral beam
and aliens smiled on us
and Jesus was there
with lamb under arm
and he anointed our heads
        blessing
and Buddha showed up and we rubbed his stomach
in pastoral mountain range
and all around bees hummed in the lavender
where eighty-seven golden virgins danced
beneath Saturn's rings
naked beatnik intoning poems
and your big blue car waiting with doors thrown open
to take us back to Earth
where we became fruitful
and multiplied
and all of them—

the saints, the gods, the sinners, and the poets—
all of them watch
and they say
"It is good."

Leave Together

Friday, my father screaming
that you're standing me up—
drunk already at 11:30.

Racing in your Oldsmobile
to get to me in time
I pace in front of our new apartment and wait
no one stands with me
no one brings me flowers for my hair.

Garden courthouse
giant clock on a brick wall
marking time
roses in an arbor, pink and full
suffocated with vines
your mother's dress
and your sister's new hat.

Everyone's faces set and grim
the words spill over me
like cool water
your hands clutch me like a dying man
I sweat and slip in your grasp
stutter out the words, whisper
promise, forever, always
drowning while they watch us
in disapproval
the sun burns and
turns my hair into a halo of fire
your tie quietly chokes you.

In the parking lot we turn away
from all of them
another couple is waiting
her belly sticks out 9 months worth
white dress pulled up in the front
to show her white plastic sandals
her girls pass her a cigarette
she huffs and laughs
loitering like I did

was it only fifteen minutes ago?
the groom stands next to his Camaro
in black jeans and boots.

The used car lot next door is having a sale,
flags jerk in the summer wind.
I stop and look at you over the top of the car
this time we go home together.

A year in the life...

A summer night
stars creamy in the velvet dark.
Your hand snakes toward mine
darkened porch
the chilly clatter of bike wheels
from the sidewalk—
a memory as we watch the silent street.

Autumn turns the wind to first frost,
and the children wear coats in the yard.
The walk sleeps, obliterated by yellow leaves
costumed kids rush to the door
capes streaming
pushing their plastic pumpkins up,
bumping and jostling each other to be first.
I lean over the steps and drop sweets to them
breathe in their candy scent.

Winter comes and whisks the leaves away,
leaving the street barren.
Inside the house
smells of garlic and tomato
you in a chair
lights and a decorated tree—
Allen is practicing his instrument;
there is no reason to ever leave here.

And now it's spring,
and a wild crocus is blooming in the yard.
The sun comes through fresh green canopy to warm the porch
unfound Easter eggs brighten
shadowed corners
I step out into the warmth
the sweet and stinging smell of grass—
hurry to where the boys call my name.

Up to you

I'm crying now
but that's a normal state for me
a mother's love is never done
never dormant
never waiting
hung like an albatross slung around our necks
from first eye twinkle
to when they handed over your ashes
and on
and on
the heart beats on
your cells inside me
til death and on
we're each other's ride or die
we're committed now
locked eternally
and the pregnancy resource center never listed this
as one of the potential side effects of
giving birth
they mentioned pain
but not like this
not this soul-searing
middle of the night
screaming
dreams of a lion
silently stalking me
or dreams where you come back
and stand in the kitchen
wearing a jean jacket
and a forgiving smile
and if I had known
I would have taken it all
all of that and more
and gladly

that is mother heart-love
that endures for you
for me
they can't separate us
even now.

In the Family Way

Black, snowy horizon, necessitating change.
If we went to Prague, what then?
stumbling around in a darkness not unlike this one
one difference - no one speaks so I can understand-
New York, too expensive, too explosive, no air or light
babies need both
and a lot more.
What can one expect from poet parents?
Upheaval constant change confusion   chaos
love passion literature travel
a storybook childhood
but you'll probably end up in therapy
No one taught me how to be your mother!
so forgive my errors in judgment-
I was meant to be a writer of poems
but I've ended up a writer of you, of your life.
We did the easy part, now it's your turn
to write the next chapter.
Oh, I hope you don't fall down and break
your glasses.
I hope you don't listen to the voice in your head,
the one that says you're not enough
I hope the voice doesn't sound like me.

The Shape of a Man

We're baking bread,
my young blonde son and I
and the yeasty smell is rising up into our noses
and we're giggling and fondling
the warm alive breathing stuff
he is standing on Mickey Mouse stool
leaning his head back into me,
pressing his hands in the firm dough
he can't say bread, yet

can't reconcile this w/the finished product
but he can feel this
hopefully remember forever.

This is what will make him a man,
kneading female food with our fingers,
shaping it and loving it with our palms.

Alone

Your children's pictures: sweet child cheeks lined up along your desk
like little soldiers
School age innocence captured and displayed with endless
gap-toothed wonderment and Garanimal stripes
But remember:
we are all alone,
these families are a short-term solution to a long term problem.

We are born alone, we die alone
our souls brought to the angels alone
on clouds with harps and golden halos
or to Inferno riding nuclear missile like wild Dr. Strangelove Texan nightmare
or to the nothingness that exists in the place of never was.

We dream alone, at night in our marriage bed
we sleep alone, some nights: husband at work, college, concert, stupor,
or affair
we drive alone, in the car, on our way somewhere
and it strikes us like a fist, middle of the solar plexus:
lonely
and we cry out
for a child, a lover, a friend
to find us
on this lonesome road and bring us home
to light, to love
to sweet child cries,
to the smell of soup and bread on the table
to our mothers and fathers, dead though they are
to the place inside ourselves that we forgot around 6th grade
that place of magic and wonder,
where we can dream in fields of autumn sunshine
golden birch rain on our baby heads
North Country fantasies and celestial breath
when we gave ourselves the freedom to dream, to watch parents kiss in the
kitchen
to hide in the backseat of the car and pretend that we are invisible
riders, counting the telephone poles that are really sleeping giants
to never be alone
to dream of never being alone again
to always have a hand, clutched in yours

as you walk up the library steps
in a new millennium
as you type at your desk and look into their faces
those children,
kindergarten babies
who will rip your heart out
leave you alone at the playground when they find someone new
skip away from your hugs, first day of school,
forsake you at graduation to go in search of their friends
who will walk away from you toward college dorm, and not look back
leave early in a car from their wedding
can't wait to leave you
can't wait to leave you

can't wait to leave you
alone.

Family Bed

You're waking up now
with tiny mewling cries.
Oh, god, it's only been 45 minutes.
I stumble over to peer at your waking face in shadowy cradle,
whisper, "It's not time yet"
your tiny fist waves in the air like a true
        revolutionary.
I pick you up,
you sigh against my shoulder,
half-heartedly suck my skin as I carry you to bed
where we lay like lovers in the moonlight,
your faced tipped toward mine,
eyes tight shut and mouth wide open
searching
I settle back and watch the shadows revolve around the room.
It's 4:47 am.
We are sentinels with you
        between us.
You kick and hit w/flailing limbs
or tickle with sharp fingers and toes;
we keep you safe
for now
the best we can do.

Lovage

far from their bombed out country
they create an oasis
choke berries aronia
and lovage
a giant tree bursting with yellow apples
dark burgundy chrysanthemums
planted for the dead

Here, where their car was stolen
and they barely speak the language
they've built something, forged ahead
grown son, tall and strong,
has come home to visit
mother cannot stop gazing at his face
cannot stop stroking his arm
his knee

her eyes find mine
guilty
with love
she has her boy
I have the moon.

She has old country recipes
for soup to heal my heart
because she knows to lose a country is to lose a son
and to lose a son
is to commit cellular level genocide
flee across an ocean

A sprig of thyme
the pork chop I made you that night
our countries were wild and we long for them
despite the wars, the tears, the grief of mothers
the difference is she will return some day
home to her garden where lovage grows 7 feet

Her son digs some up for me
to plant it in your garden
where it can grow

wild and tall
like you

if it is all I have
I will make soup
enough to find my way home again.

Middle aged practicality

Your bare foot in the dark
sharing Chinese food out of a white paper carton
watching music videos all night
sitting together at tiny desk with impossible knees pulled up
teacher pointing to crayon drawings like Dead Sea scrolls
changing a tire, side of anonymous interstate
side by side at welfare office, rushing out to throw up in green-tiled bathroom
nodding through endless middle school band concerts
the sweat behind your knees in southern hazy morning as you load the car
strawberry ice cream and bacon
Pacific waves with your arm around my waist
the deafening sound of a silent ambulance
Canyons of LA
lost in Kentucky
drunk in Kalamazoo
broke in a diner and slipping out the side door when no one's looking
drive-thrus and drive-ins
popcorn dropped between the seats
eggs smashed into the upholstery

Still finding poetry in each other
even when you think it's lost.

Summer Morning

I.
Heavy and waiting
bloated, beached
summer air hot and still   as peaches
a breeze a wish a whisper a hope—
you were born on a day like this
eyes like sheets flapping in the wind
fingers like onions half cooked in a pan
veins so baby so bloody so blue
scary with need and eagerness
reaching out with
pursed mouth
angry and flailing
pushed out into the heat of
summer morning   mewling
you drank the tepid air, burped,
sighed.

I drive with you in the car,
front seat now
sweat pooling under and around us
your hand flies through
the air of the open window
imagining spaceship, pirate's ship,
an airplane to take you far from me
knees scraped raw,
glasses slightly crooked
t-shirt stained with chocolate ice cream
a summer boy
thoughts of baseball
your heat radiates out to me.

II.
You died on a day like this
a day the sun refused to stop
relentlessly beating
no clouds
a sunrise that would break your heart
if it wasn't already broken

dawn coming slow
over familiar downtown
while in air conditioned hospital
a quarter century circle neatly closed
around my throat
born on the 3rd floor
died on the 1st
and I never saw the 2nd floor
but I imagine it isn't anything special either.

Your shirt
and hat
and shoes
your car
and wallet
and driver's license
your gray socks
pulled on without thought
hours before
and all the pain your heart could bear
and more more more.

I wasn't there
and it haunts me
I felt your first breath
but not the last
I know you don't mind
but I do
sweet child cheeks
sweet innocent wild baby
sweet summer boy
your music still spreads like a heartbeat
through the house.

Moving Day

Our little house of fights and failures
a soon-to-be distant memory
walls repainted
carpets pulled up
Christmas morning children
hot chocolate and cinnamon rolls
stale Halloween candy mashed into
heat register
grimy refrigerator handle
light spilling out into
midnight kitchen
someone else's bare feet
as they stand and stare
looking for cold chicken
sick babies crying in cribs
lost, lonely socks
thunderstorm porch swing
red maple's golden leaves
piling up over steps
the streetlight that shines
through bedroom window
the sound of the shower
I will pack it all up
shove it into boxes
and bags
haul it out to the trunk
buckle it in
all of it
and you
and the children.
We will all go together
We will make new.

Empty

I am empty
and I cry for the babies that fell
from my belly,
that I scooped up and pressed and fed
I am empty
and the babies are gone
torn from my breasts
and out flying a goddamned kite
in the spring evening air
away and away and far far away
on the other edge of
pink-scalloped dusk
suckles them now
and breathes her breath onto their rosy
cheeks and
pets their golden boy-heads and
praises their name
like I used to.
I am empty,
the wicked witch in the gingerbread house
waiting for the children to come and eat my soul
my sex is useless to me now
the babies simply flow out red and laughing
my breasts are rioting in a way I don't like
they threaten and will revolt in black cancer
my insides turn out for the world to see
and sneer at
and the stars turn
on
my whispering voice calls the children home
I can almost hear the kite flap in the distance
hear the deathly silence that is future.

Looking Toward Future—21st Century

I.

Next thing you know
you're old, broken
low-rent Charles Bukowski
sad
and sagging
everywhere
before you've had a chance to do
anything.

That's how they want to keep you
down and out
and standing in endless lines
around the corner and down
past the parking garages
until you've forgotten what you're waiting for.
And no one cares what you've read
or whom you've met
or what you wrote once on a napkin
in a bar
your genius so prolific
you could wad it up and throw it out
on your way home.

II.

I dream, unfocused on reams of messiest poetry
as Tim mutters about Michael McClure
in the corner, by the bookshelf
our precious child long since
run off
to write books of his own about lousy parents
cockroach scurries across green linoleum
while I'm on the toilet
another empty bottle,
rolls on its own
across my line of vision
When will my lace bird curtains fly away?

III.

Bleak imagined future
where does it come from and why now?
with cute sleeping boy in baby swing
with Big Bird grinning at me
with burning cigarette end almost at my fingers
with dark green furniture
with candles lit and pretty
with Chicago this weekend
with pot looming next week
with bills piling up
with cracked new notebook
on lap
with Whitman, with Wakowski
with blues so close I can taste them
with Tim
"You're morbid and cute,"
he says
then kisses my toes while I shrink.

US Highway 94

Hurtling through the darkness with you
the children on our backs
past dune towns and winter woods
car lights spark
the warmth of your hand
your arm in kelly green wool cardigan
billboards splash their garish colors across your cheeks
on our way home to light
your lips
your hands rest light on the steering wheel
this is love
this is love
a car of love
flashing through a night without stars
the boys breathe in and out all the way down the freeway
the windows are foggy
life
seeps in through cold glass
the tires pulse with every mile
the radio serves harmonica
I exhale poetry and
your hands
veins
bones
muscles
      skin

Untitled

These days I lean
I lean against walls and counters
count my breaths
trying to gather the strength of upright again
until I can move on
walk down the hall - open the bathroom door
finish making dinner

I lean against fences staring through slats at happy families
at children on trampolines
at an old couple manning a barbecue
and I think too much
and then I go home

I lean against memories
furious ones that come with no warning
unexpected and sharp
or the slow ones that come on like a cold
I let the waves pound until
I can move again

I lean against dad
even while he's leaning against me
we hold each other up with equal and opposite force
like we always have

I lean into the wind
tell myself it's your breath on my cheek
your voice in my ear
that I'll see you again soon
when we both know that's a beautiful little lie
that I can lean on
if only for a minute or two.

The tree limbs in the backyard bend and snap in the wind
this spring
our first without you
and the buds come slow and maybe they're a brighter green--
but who am I to say.

For Allen

Born of feminism and punk rock
eyes that fill at the slightest affront
chin that quivers when you try not to cry
and I am abashed
when I speak to you harshly
you live in a cave of adolescence
protected by your earbuds
loud clanging music that echoes through the evening
while you sit and do your homework
and suck down chocolate at your desk
I linger in the hallway outside your room
afraid for you
I see the man you will be
sarcastic and silly
wrapped up in your own insecurities
and alone as men tend to be
you're all wrapped up in skin and bones and
falling out teeth
you're all wrapped up like a present
someone gave me long ago
that I looked at and loved and put back in the box
to keep safe
soon someone will open the box and take you out
she will unwrap you from the tissue paper
and marvel at your clean shiny newness
she will thank me,
I think.

I hate 4 in the morning.

It smells of pee and cold air,
Sticky menthol on your chest,
stomach aches in the night
bad dreams and children
crying out from their beds.
It is on-the-way-to-work
early morning dead streets
streetlights sad sorrow
cold shadows as you open the place
again.

It is 4am when you bolt awake with jolting fear gripping you--
the car payment late again
and the yellow flashing lights of the tow truck
outside your window.
4 in the morning is when you roll over
realize you don't know the man next to you any more
when you get up, out of bed, go to the closet and fill the suitcase
leave a note or
don't.

It's 4 something when they leave the voice mail
you won't get until 6,
the nurse's voice soft but ominous
get here quick
        get here now
but it's too late
too late

No matter what time the clock says
it is always 4 am when the call comes.
Death and birth at the same hour,
when you rush to the car, panting,
when you squeeze a pillow between your knees
to keep him in until you get to the hospital
when you pull up screeching in front of the emergency doors
when you push him out wailing into 4am predawn pre-millennium time warp
future.

Our Job

Our job is to stay put
be cool
not rock the boat
keep the home fires burning indefinitely
make sure everything stays the same,
so when they come
and open your dresser drawers
the smell of you
rises to meet
and catapults them
back
to whatever teenage memory
they cherish.

Our job
is to hold them tight
let them cry
feed them
make sure the candles and incense stay
lit
listen to the stories again
and play your records for them.

Our job is to pretend that we don't
imagine
their headlights pulling into the driveway
are yours
to hide the inevitable truth
when we open the door
and you're not standing there
and you never will again.

New

I just want to live a patient life
with clothes out on a line
I just want to run away
from everything
and from you
and from you
          from you

from you

You
are
always there
looking at my faults
judging all the things
I haven't got to yet
not yet
(maybe never)
disconnect the phone
pay the bill too late
putting things back
in the grocery store
without enough money to pay
find a greenish penny
on the closet floor
alarm clock set wrong
and I'm late again
where the fuck are my keys
what's that smell
and all the boys on the bus cry
and all the boys on the street cry
and all the boys on the
on the way home
they cry
their tears a hot ocean
and I can float in the middle like a desert island
float all the way back to myself
look at me inside the mirror
and once I was little and I liked to play paper dolls
and once I was little and I had long braids

once I was little and I could forget
but now I'm big and now I'm big and now and now and now
it's time to grow up.

April

leaving
our shitty apartment building
on our way to work minimum wage jobs
cold but sunny
and our neighbors pulling
SSI checks from mass mailboxes
we didn't have a TV
no smart phones or computer
the newspaper box outside
proclaimed Kurt was dead
you fumbled for the quarter or whatever it cost back then
newsprint staining your fingers black
as a concert t-shirt
later we watched Courtney read the suicide note
to an army of flannel freaks just like us
cried as one.

Three years later
in the break room of a different shitty job
that smelled like soup and moldy carpet
eating a sandwich and calculating my overtime pay
someone left a newspaper on the table
and just like that, Allen Ginsberg was dead
while our Allen was home and three years old
wearing corduroy pants, a t-shirt
and learning how to read.

Your dad died in April too.

April deaths glitter in new grass like dangerous bombs

We almost lost Allen in April
a day before easter
rushing to the hospital
to find him sitting up in bed watching baseball
customary chagrin
and a plastic bag with a t-shirt they had to cut off him
to save his life
so yeah, April can fuck off.

Comparison

Perhaps unwise to compare
two blonde boys
blue or brown-eyed boys
born in summer
with long limbs and stretching toes
best not to linger on thoughts of firsts
rolling over
walking
chattered words
and who sang what song
in the backseat of the car
cannot compare
report cards
and genuine clumsy athletic ability
dramatic or mellow
theatrical or musical
only want to have them both here
to reach over our table
for the last dinner roll.

The Virus #1
April 2020

Last night / I dreamt it was The End / and you and I were sledding down the middle of 28th Street / in a fine snow / the kind that's like sugar / tiny crystals to fill up your nose and lungs / the garden store and the baby store and the Dollar Tree / empty and dark / no need for potted plants and infant layettes and cheap wrapping paper / distractions gone / deserted / five lanes unplowed before us / Steak N' Shake / Circuit City.

You gave us a tremendous push / and hopped on behind me as we gained momentum/ a ghost wind chapped our cheeks /we glided alone / small red sled / into the uncertain future.

Meanwhile

Without all of you
there's no music
sifting down from punk rock attic haven
or wafting up from make-shift basement pirate radio
8-bit jangle from video game machine
silent lonely kitchen
no one harassing me to change stations
chiding me on my musical tastes
no one sings in the shower
or strums on the couch
the same guitar chord
       over   and   over
no one practices playing "Dixie"
       on   the   keyboard
no one makes up silly songs
and dances in their underpants
to make me laugh
as if I'm special somehow
as if my laughter somehow makes you more alive.

Everything's Broken

Grief sits at my dinner table every night and gorges on
stir fry and tacos and roasted potatoes
grief plays on the radio
every song
jazz and country
rock and roll most of all
Dylan and Louis Jordan and Little Richard
and the Ramones - I don't switch it off
because that might make you retreat haunt someone else but maybe
that's not how it works maybe
you stay around because I'm broken maybe
you're trying to help maybe
you're waiting to see
          if I can pull it together enough
to mend what's broken
I'd like to think you still have faith in me
still think (if you are capable of thought)
that if anyone can fix this, I can.
But this is unfixable
this thing is totaled
run off the rails
and if there is a "next"
          if there is an "after"
it will still have a huge gash, a crack
as deep and as dark as 4 AM
as deep as love
as dark as time
a new thing
developed out of shattered pieces
created from love and despair
maybe I'll give it a name
the poor misshapen lump
the freaky thing that crawls onto my lap
maybe I'll feed it roasted potatoes and pet it sometimes
maybe it will turn its blind eyes to me
with something like love
like grace.

Failures

All the ways I've tried and failed
crowd around me
all the tiny little cancers fill up my brain with black blight
all the times I turned on the TV
lay with the baby on the couch exhausted
thought "this is your life now."
when we listened in bed with exhaustion and shame to
cockroaches beginning their nightly dance
when we ate ramen noodles and hamburger helper every night
or fed the kids something boxed or microwaved
all the jobs tried for and rejected
all the poems unwritten and free-floating
all the trips planned for and then forgotten
all the glorious golden stretching afternoons
with nothing to do in hot summer sunshine
never once did I think that one day I would wish myself back there
notes unsent
calls I wish I could make
to numbers no longer in service
walking home through blue blanket twilight
with cold lips and fingers
the many times I stopped and thought "I will remember this
        for the rest of my life"
        I can't remember. Can we consider that failure?

*We had ceiling shadows that made shapes for us in the dark —him and her—
they made love all night long above us in orange relief as we lay awake.
The trees were thick and green, our apartment deep and shady.*

Contagious

It's not contagious—
my dead son
won't
corrupt your living children
your doe-eyed babies
my grief can't wrap
itself around your perfect family
like invasive ivy
and pull you apart at the seams
this loss of mine
won't twist its way in
kick your door down
the damage is already done
and I am living proof
no matter how much you want to die
your lungs keep filling with air
your legs keep walking
your heart, although missing,
still continues to beat
even when you wish it would stop.

Untitled

      A baby smells good
all the time--
when he's clean
shiny and skin warm
rosy and clinging wet to your neck or
when he's dirty
with the smell of sun
bright on the back of his head
sweat in the sweet folds
dirt between his fingers
as he squashes it in his fat fist.

Like This

I do not fear death
not anymore—
I fear boredom
without constant distraction
thoughts run amok
to places I don't want to go
and I fear sleeplessness
night churning around me
stomach dissolving insomnia pills
into uselessness
and the way the light creeps around my bedroom
while dad and dog snore
I fear conflict
and anger and harsh words
but also unexpected kindnesses
both assaults that I don't know what to do with.

I fear music—
every new song on the radio
a body blow to absorb
a memory bomb
that ticks while I fumble with the button
trying to find something harmless.
But that doesn't work either
because you always were the car DJ,
the music nazi,
clicking George Michael and Donna Summer off within one note,
giving me a look, a sigh.

I don't fear death
but I fear old age's
gentle onslaught of forgetfulness—
who will remember the feel of your four-year-old hand
and who will keep the secrets only I know
the baby secrets the boy secrets
the buzz of you.

I'm a coward who wants it to be easy
go to sleep and not wake up
the way the gruesome little kid prayer says—

if I die before I wake—
but the broken pieces of me lay scattered
across Route 66
and there's no one left to wear the glasses
that came in the mail on Friday
and who will remember Monday is garbage day
and who will fill out the paperwork
and who will remember your brother's shoe size
and dad's blood type
and what side the gas tank is on

And so the fear is life
and breath
and putting one foot in front of the other
it tastes like your favorite foods
the ones you'll never eat again
it sounds like Muddy Waters, the MC5 and
dad screaming
in the backyard at 2am
it smells like candle wax, lilacs and musty old Converse

Fear lives here now
taunting us from the shadows
pokes us and jeers and teases us
we set a place for it at the table
we welcome it in every night
beg it to leave in the morning

I don't fear death
but I do fear life
a life like this
going on like this
until the end.

Acknowledgments

"Alone" *Display* Issue #82, Fall 2005

About the Author

Lisa McAllister has been writing poetry and stories since she first learned how to make marks on paper with a pencil. Her debut novel *Mother's Little Helper* was published in October 2023. She lives in Grand Rapids, MI with her husband Tim and their ginormously spoiled goldendoodle Donna. She is the biological mom of two, Allen and Will, and the bonus mom of about 10 more extremely talented young musicians, artists and poets.